THE PRACTICE
OF
WUDANG
TAI CHI CHUAN

HAND FORM
PUSHING HANDS
APPLICATIONS

BY

IAN CAMERON

Acknowledgements

There are a few people I would like to thank. To Tadek Klasicki for his many years of support and for taking the falls. Also, Sally Munro, David Welsh, John Burns and everyone who has helped over the years.

I would like to mention Dan Docherty and Tong Chi Kin for their help and friendship.

Finally, to Ronnie Robinson without whose great help this book would not have been possible.

Ian Cameron

FIRST PUBLISHED 1997 by Golden Horse Classics

© Ian Cameron 1997

PHOTOGRAPHY
Hand Form
Ian Cameron   *by Ian Hogg*
Pushing Hands & Self Defence
Ian Cameron and Tadek Klasicki   *by Colin Carmichael*
All other photographs   *by Ronnie Robinson*

TECHNICAL ADVICE
Alister Liddell
DESIGN & LAYOUT
Chiron

ISBN 0 953 000 605

Printed and bound in the U.K. by Bell & Bain LTD. Scotland

Dedicated to

Moira and Craig

Chang San-Feng

Founder of Tai Chi Chuan

A SPECIAL THANKS

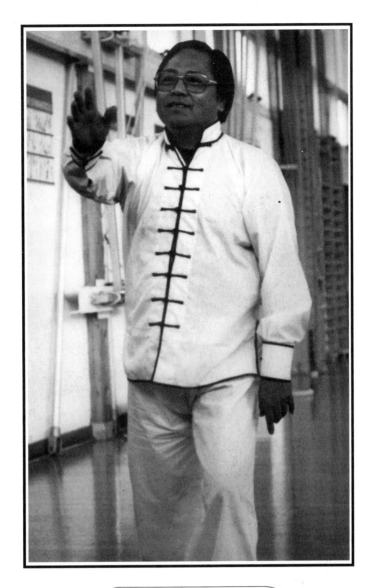

Cheng Tin Hung

I must pay a special thanks to Sifu Cheng Tin Hung for his teaching. I was extremely fortunate to have this great Tai Chi master as my teacher. He has been a great source of inspiration to me for a long time, and it is over the years that I have come to appreciate the depth of his art.

He made my family very welcome when we lived in Hong Kong, making it a rewarding experience for us all.

When I was looking for a teacher, it was very difficult to know if you were going to receive good quality teaching. I will be forever grateful to the unknown shopkeeper who pointed me in the right direction.

Little did I know then, how Tai Chi would grow as it has done today. With the popularity, of course comes a very uneven spread of standards. It is for this reason that I am so grateful for what Sifu Cheng taught. His Tai Chi was real and very down to earth. This down to earth approach belied a tremendous talent, an ability that was second to none. Over the years of watching Tai Chi grow in the way it has, Sifu Cheng's teachings have taken on more meaning as time has gone on. It was a great pleasure for us to have Sifu Cheng stay at our home when he paid his visits to the UK. My students benefitted greatly from his teaching.

In a Tai Chi world that has masters round every corner, it has meant so much to me to have been in the company of the real thing.

FOREWORD

Ian Cameron learned Tai Chi from Sifu Cheng Tin Hung in Hong Kong in the early 1970's. Since that time he has been one of the most important figures in British Tai Chi, making sure that the Tai Chi that is passed on to his students is the genuine article, imbued with the spirit of the art as he learned it.

I first started working with Ian in 1979 and, since then, have had the pleasure of watching his Tai Chi deepen into a very subtle and powerful art that is a constant source of wonder to all who see it.

Yet, it is as a teacher that Ian stands out most. His movements are so clear that he makes it very easy for his students to follow, though he has always made it clear that copying the teacher's external movement is only the beginning. To master the art the student must go beyond the shape of the postures and continually explore their internal significance.

In this, Ian is a marvellous teacher, always available to his students, patient, open and generous in his sharing of the art. Students of all levels are tactfully guided towards new levels of appreciation of the vastness of Tai Chi in ways that benefit them, and will ultimately benefit the art as well. If Tai Chi is to develop in the West it will only do so in the hands of a teacher like Ian Cameron who teaches a Tai Chi filled with the vigorous spirit of the 'true men of old.'

John Burns

CONTENTS

PREFACE

Sifu Cheng Tin Hung's Tai Chi Chuan is descended from the lineage of Yang Lu Chan and through his second son, Yang Pan Hau.

Wu Chan Yu, a Manchurian, was taught by both these masters. This was the beginning of the Wu family lineage.

Wu Chien Chuan, son of Wu Chan Yu, is recognised as the founder of the Wu style of Tai Chi Chuan. This style is second only to the Yang style in popularity.

Cheng Win Kwong was a student of Wu Chien Chuan and, in turn, passed his art on to his nephew, Cheng Tin Hung.

Cheng Tin Hung had another teacher, a Buddhist by the name of Chai Man Hun who was a very strict Master. So strict that he lost many of his students. At one time Cheng Tin Hung was his only remaining student. This Master was responsible for Cheng Tin Hung's deepening understanding of the theoretical and fighting aspects of Tai Chi Chuan.

Today the Tai Chi Chuan passed on by Cheng Tin Hung is named Wudang Tai Chi Chuan. This is simply named after the mountain range where the founder, Chang San Feng lived.

Ian Cameron

INTRODUCTION

I first started to practice Tai Chi Chuan with Grandmaster Cheng Tin Hung in 1971 in Hong Kong. It was while I was there with the armed forces that I decided to make the best use of my time and follow up an interest in the Martial Arts. Tai Chi had, up to that point, been something that I had just seen in a few books, and now was the opportunity to learn more about it. It has now been twenty-five years and I'm still learning more about it.

Over the past two decades Tai Chi has become increasingly popular. Even though this is the case, it is still a very much misunderstood art. It is essential therefore, when learning, that students be given the correct information and method, so that they can make steady progress through the various aspects of Tai Chi.

The true roots of Tai Chi Chuan are in the Martial Arts of ancient China. Chang San Feng, the founder of Tai Chi, was already a master of the various martial methods used in the Shaolin Temple. What he discovered was, that although very effective, they all relied largely on speed and strength. Being himself a Taoist, he began to evolve a system based on the principle of Yin and Yang, this is actually called Tai Chi. The word, 'Chuan' means fist. So Tai Chi Chuan is the Martial Art based upon this principle.

Tai Chi

Tai Chi has always been renowned for its therapeutic benefits and is practiced by many people for this purpose alone. It is due largely to its success in this area that some of the martial aspects have been neglected. It is not wrong to say that Tai Chi is for one's health, although I know of no Martial Art that isn't used to protect one's health. I'm not advocating that students should practice for the purpose of knocking people around, far from it. Tai Chi is a complete art and it should, as far as possible, be understood in its entirety. It is the responsibility of the teacher to help the student reach his or her potential, therefore it is important that the teacher has a deep knowledge and understanding of Tai Chi. This means that he must not only be able to pass on the forms and understand the movements, but also know thoroughly the theory and philosophy that lies behind the art of Tai Chi Chuan. The Yin and Yang principle is expressed here by knowing both the physical and the intellectual aspects. How is it possible to pass on an art if only a small part is known?

Tai Chi can have positive effects on daily life, not only due to the improvement of one's health but also in dealing with everyday situations. By using the principles of Yin and Yang many problems can be overcome. For example: an attack can be verbal as well as physical. When something of this nature arises, it is better to listen; accept what is said, if true. If not, then after hearing the other person's point of view, you can explain your side of things. By listening, you are yielding, and not just waiting to have an argument. Yielding must not be seen as giving in. On the contrary; it is a way of accepting situations as they are and dealing with them in a calm and controlled manner. To resist is to simply indulge in a trial of strength, whether this be verbal or physical. Using Yin and Yang in this way can relieve much of the stress which is one of the most common causes of illness in society today.

Tai Chi can be practiced on many levels. This entirely depends upon the individual and to what extent he or she wishes to practice. Tai Chi can be as arduous as any other Martial Art, and it takes a great deal of time and effort to progress to the point where one is competent in every aspect of the art. This is where a competent master is important. It is unfortunate but true, that much of the Tai Chi taught today is inferior. This is due mainly to teachers who haven't taken the time to learn the art properly before trying to pass it on. Tai Chi is very deceptive in that it looks easy to do but is in fact difficult to do well. It has been said in the past that nothing can make up for natural ability, but great progress can be made with diligent practice. This is a very important point.

If one is practicing for health reasons, the forms and pushing hands will be sufficient and one's general health will be improved with regular practice. However, if one wishes to take things further it is necessary to undertake a prolonged period of training lasting many years. Even when one is competent, the practice must continue, complacency is something to be avoided. True Tai Chi, as I understand it, is a tough and demanding regime. Many stories tell of the harshness of some of the old masters, who weren't all the gentle sage-like characters that some people today imagine them to be. Maybe not all gentlemen, but all expert in Tai Chi. The outer shapes of the forms can be learned fairly quickly. However, it takes practice over many years to really get to know the true depths of Tai Chi.

Although everything is repetition, it is this that is the key to further improvement in Tai Chi. It is possible to learn Tai Chi quickly but, it is the long hours of continual practice that really matter. The truth is, you cannot do the same movement twice. Each time you raise your hands it is a new movement. Practiced in this way training is always fresh and creative. Most people experience stale periods where no feeling of improvement is apparent. Good attitude is important to go beyond this point and encourage the 'spirit' to carry on. The only way that progress will be made is to continually keep this motivation strong. One way to avoid this is not to look for anything, then no dissatisfaction will arise from not achieving an aim. You really can only be where you are and results will come from constant practice. Practice for its own sake. With this kind of attitude towards Tai Chi even the most complex movement becomes simpler. Finally, everyone must come to their own understanding of Tai Chi. This is only possible through hard work and diligent practice, only you can do this.

HOW TO USE THIS BOOK

What is shown here is what is called the square form Each movement is clearly defined so that the proper structure of the form can be learned. This form is like printing, when one is learning to write. Once this has been learned and the student is comfortable with it, he then goes on to learn the round form, which is like long hand. To carry this analogy a little further, each person develops their own style of writing and the same is also true of Tai Chi. This simply means that no two people move in the same way and this will show when performing the Tai Chi form.

Starting from the posture, The Tai Chi Beginning Style, the moves should be counted in groups of three. Any connecting movement will be indicated by (A) or (B).

It is difficult to convey a sense of movement through the use of photographs, this is why Tai Chi should always be taught by a competent master and books used only as an aid to memory.

POINTS TO REMEMBER

1)   Have patience when learning.

2)   Learn the postures thoroughly.

3)   Pay attention to your posture.

4)   Make sure you are facing in the correct direction.

5)   Practice at home what you are taught in the class.

6)   Keep watching more experienced Tai Chi players.

7)   Ask if you are not sure.

THE HAND FORM

The most widely known and practiced aspect of Tai Chi is the solo hand form. To practice this form is to learn to relax the body in a particular way. That is, by paying close attention to the posture, and keeping this correct, the muscles will be able to relax in a natural way. Relaxation does not mean that the muscles are flaccid but that they must always have tone.

The *'Ready Stance'* (fig. 1) which begins the Tai Chi sequence is an opportunity to check out the posture before starting the form. Keep the feet shoulder width apart, i.e. the outside of the feet in line with the shoulders. This is the ideal way in which the legs support the whole body. This support should be felt from the soles of the feet up to the top of the head.

When in a forward stance the knees should always be over the foot and shouldn't go beyond the toes. When in a back stance the buttocks should never extend over the heel. It is also important not to tilt the hips. Apart from causing tension in the lower back and throwing the whole posture out, it is impossible for the waist to turn properly.

The shoulders should be relaxed downwards, 'sunk' or 'hanging' would be a close approximation of how it should feel. By allowing this to happen the chest is then made concave and the back convex. This eliminates the over-arching of the lower back, which is a common fault. All of the above points should be taken note of while in the ready stance.

A further use of this posture is to take time to allow the mind and body to 'settle,' also allowing the breath to become calm. This facilitates the correct attitude before starting the form itself. Remember that the Ready Stance is part of the form.

When starting to move, the joints should be felt to be 'open and loose,' this helps towards relaxing and the form feeling comfortable. It takes time to learn to relax and it is an ongoing process, as is the continual refining of the forms. Relaxing and refining of the forms run parallel, each being a by-product of the other.

With prolonged practice, you become acutely aware of your body movements and where your tensions are. There is no need to struggle with these tensions, just acknowledge them and continue to practice in as relaxed a manner as possible. No matter how relaxed one feels, there is always a little corner that doesn't feel quite right. The same rule applies, acknowledge it and carry on. Continual practice reduces these tensions.

Coordination is something that is highlighted during the practice of Tai Chi. When a movement is done quickly, as in most sports, there is hardly any notice taken of the coordination required. Only when an action is slowed down, as in the hand form, does one become aware of the balance, the shift from one movement to the next, what the hands and feet are doing in relation to one another and the timing of the movements.

The body should be seen as a coordinated whole, this is where Tai Chi gets its power from, the body moving as a unit. Although the form is done in a slow and relaxed way, there is a definite physical and mental focus required to give the form content. If either is missing, the mind wandering, or part of the body pointing in the wrong direction, then posture is weakened.

When the Tai Chi Classics say, "From the feet, up the legs, directed by the waist, over the shoulders and expressed in the hands." It can simply be describing how to coordinate the body. There are many sayings that can be seen in this light. Coordination also means combining internal and external, stillness and movement, softness and firmness etc. Combining internal and external means the outer aspect i.e. the form, should be comfortable and the internal i.e. the breath, should naturally become one with the external movement. Essentially, it is movement that you are training and the breath should become a natural part of that movement. This feeling of being comfortable will take time.

To combine stillness and movement means the outer movement is to be balanced by the stillness of the mind. This doesn't mean that the mind becomes a blank, but totally immersed in the form. In the Tai Chi Classics this is called "Internalising the Spirit." Although there may be some distraction, do not let the mind get caught up with it, just keep coming back to the form.

BREATHING IN TAI CHI CHUAN

The breathing method used in Tai Chi is natural. This is achieved by using the diaphragm. Normally it is the intercostal muscles between the ribs that are used. By using the diaphragm the lungs are expanded downwards. This method uses the full capacity of the lung, thus increasing the flow of blood to the extremities.

Breathing, using the diaphragm, means that when you inhale the abdomen expands outwards and when you exhale the abdomen contracts. This type of breathing gives the stomach muscles a chance to move in such a way as not only to strengthen them, but to benefit the internal organs.

However, there should be no forcing of the breath. By using the posture described previously, the breath will naturally be developed. There are two aspects in breathing which are of some importance. They are: thinking the breath to be long and thin, also keeping the breath fine, this means it should be quiet. You should breathe deeply to the Tan Tien (1.5 - 2" below the navel.) which is the physical centre of the body. This facilitates the concept of 'sinking' which is important to the development of good Tai Chi.

During the practice of Tai Chi the emphasis is placed on relaxing the whole body and having a tranquil mind. Through constant practice of natural breathing the breath will become deep, slow and soft. All the organs of the body are in harmony using this system.

Remember, it is important that there is no effort in trying to artificially combine the breathing with the movements of the form.

THE HAND FORM

Ready Stance
Relax the shoulders, keeping the body naturally erect and the feet shoulder width apart. The palms are facing downwards.

Tai Chi Beginning Style
1) Raise the hands to shoulder height.

2) Drop the elbows bringing the hands back towards the shoulder.

3) Take the hands down, returning them to their original position.

1) Sink down bending the knees.

2) With the weight on the right, step forward from the knee with the left foot, placing the heel on the ground.

3) Raise up the left hand circling it until the palm is facing you.

1) Raise the right hand up to the right bringing it round so it is inside the left. The palms are now facing each other.

2) Draw both hands towards you and, at the same time, turn the left foot on the heel so that it is pointing to the right.

3) Shift the weight forward to the left foot, bending the left knee. At the same time the hands are pushed towards their original position.

1) Take the right hand out to the right, turning the head to follow the movement.

2) Keep the stance at the same height, raise the heel off the ground turning the body to face directly to the right.

3) Step forward placing the right heel on the ground. At the same time the hands come together with the left fingers touching the right wrist.

Grasping The Bird's Tail
1) Turn the hands so that the right hand is palm up and the left is palm down. At the same time bend forward taking the hands down in front of the body.

2) Shift the weight forward turning the waist and taking the hands out diagonally to the left. The right knee does not extend beyond the toes.

3) Remain in the same stance and turn the waist diagonally to the right.

1) Shift the weight back to the left taking the hands back slightly towards you.

2) Turn the hands so that the right hand is facing down and the left is facing up. Again take the hands down to the centre of the body.

3) Move forward so that the weight is on the right side. Take the hands up and out diagonally left. The left hand is palm up and the right is palm down.

Single Whip
1) Turn the right foot forward on the heel, at the same time the right hand turns down bringing the fingertips and thumb together.

2) Take the left foot a small step out to the left touching the toes down. Take care not to step out too far.

2A) Settle the body into the centre of the stance. The weight is equally on both feet.

3) Take the left hand across the front of the body, turning the waist to the left. As you turn the waist forward, turn the left hand, palm forward. Finally sink a little more into the stance.

Flying Oblique
1) Shift the weight to the left side allowing the right foot to turn naturally on the ball of the foot. The left hand turns up and the right hand is palm down.

Raise Hands & Step Up
2) Turn the whole body forward placing the right heel on the ground. At the same time the right hand comes round to the front, palm facing towards you.

3) Take the left hand down so that both palms are facing each other.

1) Shift the weight forward on to the right side.

2) Step in keeping the feet shoulder width apart. As you step in, straighten the body.

3) Stand up raising the right hand, palm facing out. At the same time, drop the left hand down by your side.

White Crane Flaps its Wings
1) Bend forward from the waist. Allow the left hand to come forward as you bend. Keep the legs straight and do not bend too much.

2) Using the waist, turn the upper body to the left.

3) Raise the left hand in a circular way up and round to the side of the head.

1) Raise the body up to a standing position, still facing left.

2) Turn the waist so that you are facing the front.

3) Take the hands down with the left hand facing forward. The right hand is facing towards you with the fingers pointing to the left. Keep the elbows down

Seven Stars Brush Knee Twist Step
1) Sink down, turn on the ball of the right foot so that you are facing to the left. The left hand leads and both hands are on the centre line of the body.

2) Take the hands out to the right, right hand facing in with the fingers pointing forward. The left palm faces down. Simultaneously take a small step out with the left foot.

3) Brush down with the left hand, circling in front of the body, finishing outside the line of the left leg. Let the right palm turn to face forward to complete the movement.

Seven Stars
1) Shift the weight back on to the right side

2) Drop the elbow allowing the hand to come back towards you.

3) Take the left hand up, touching the right fingers to the wrist.

Brush Knee & Twist Step
1) Raise the right hand, pointing the fingers forward.

2) Turn the waist taking the hands out to the right.

3) Repeat first Brush Knee & Twist Style.

1) Step straight forward with the right foot.

2) Raise the left hand up to the front, then turn the waist taking the hands out to the left.

3) Brush down with the right hand circling in front of the body, coming to rest outside the line of the right leg. The left hand pushes forward with the palm turning to complete the movements.

1) Step straight forward with the left foot.

2) Raise the right hand up to the front then turn the waist taking the hands out to the right.

3) Repeat first Brush Knee Twist Style.

Seven Stars
1) Shift the weight back on to the right side

2) Drop the elbow allowing the hand to come back towards you.

3) Take the left hand up, touching the right fingers to the wrist.

Stroke The Lute
1) Turn the waist to the right and face at an angle of 45°.

2) Shift the weight forward turning the hands so that the left is palm down and the right palm up.

3) Turn the waist left to an angle of 45°.

1) Still facing the same angle, step in with the right foot.

2) Bring the hands back to the centre of the body.

3) Stand up straight.

Step Up Parry and Punch
1) Step forward with the left foot. At the same time make a small circle with the hands. The circle is forwards and back to the original position.

2) Make a gentle fist with the right hand and touch it to the left palm. Turn the waist to the right. The hands circle downwards to the right.

2A) Circle the hands back and up. As they reach the point shown, start to shift the weight forward.

2B) Complete the circle by shifting the weight forward taking the hands forward to the centre line of the body.

3) Take the right fist back to the waist, shifting the weight back to the right side.

1) Turn the waist to the right, taking the left hand across the body. The left hand is outside the right hand line of the body.

2) Turn the waist back to the left, turning the left palm down.

3) Shift the weight forward, punching with the right hand. The left hand touches the inside of the elbow.

As If Shutting A Door
1) Place the left hand palm up, under the forearm.

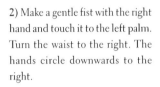

2) Shift the weight back. Take both hands up and back so that both palms are facing you.

3) Shift the weight forward, turning the hands so that the palms are facing away from you.

Embrace Tiger and Return To Mountain
1) Move the weight back slightly, at the same time turn the left foot on the heel and drop the hands straight down. Shift the weight back on to the left side.

2) Turn the body to face 45° to the right rear. As you turn also turn the hands so that the palms are facing out. The heel of the right foot touches the ground.

3) Take the weight on to the right side. At the same time the right hand comes up and the left hand is down to the left and both palms are facing forward.

Cross Hands
1) Step in with the left foot making sure that you maintain a shoulder width stance.

2) Turn the right foot from the heel to face forward, at the same time cross the hands in front, right hand on the outside.

3) Stand up straight.

Oblique Brush Knee Twist Step
1) Sink down.

2) Take a step diagonally to the left, at the same time turn the waist taking the hands out to the right.

3) Repeat previous style allowing the right foot to turn forward on the heel so that the whole body is focussed in one direction.

Turn Body Brush Knee Twist
1) Turn the left foot on the heel, at the same time the left hand comes up and round so that both palms are facing each other.

2) Keep both hands out to the left as you turn 180° to the opposite angle and step out to the right.

3) Repeat previous style. Again the foot turns on the heel to point in the direction of the focus.

Seven Stars
1) Shift the weight back to the left side.

2) Bend the left arm bringing the hand slightly towards you.

3) Place the right hand on top of the left.

Grasping The Bird's Tail
1) Turn the hands so that the right hand is palm up and the left is palm down. At the same time bend forward taking the hands down in front of the body.

2) Shift the weight forward turning the waist and taking the hands out diagonally to the left. The right knee does not extend beyond the toes.

3) Remain in the same stance and turn the waist diagonally to the right.

1) Shift the weight back to the left taking the hands back slightly towards you.

2) Turn the hands so that the right hand is facing down and the left is facing up. Again take the hands down to the centre of the body.

3) Move forward so that the weight is on the right side. Take the hands up and out diagonally left. The left hand is palm up and the right is palm down.

Oblique Single Whip
1) Turn the right foot forward on the heel, at the same time the right hand turns down bringing the fingertips and the thumb together.

2) Take the left foot a small step out to the left touching the toes down. Take care not to step out too far.

2A) Settle the body into the centre of the stance. The weight is equally on both feet.

3) Take the left hand across the front of the body, turning the waist to the left. As you turn the waist forward turn the left hand palm forward. Finally sink a little more into the stance.

Fist Under Elbow
1) Turn on the left heel until it is facing directly behind you. The left hand extends in the same direction as the foot.

2) Turn the body round making sure the right foot is parallel with the left. The right hand touches the left with the palm facing the ground.

3) Sit back, closing both hands into fists. The right hand is placed beneath the left elbow. The left hand comes back slightly towards you.

Step Back To Repulse The Monkey
1) Turn the waist to the right. Once you reach 45° shift the weight forward and open the left hand, palm facing up.

1A) Continue turning the waist until the left hand is in a straight line with the shoulder.

2) Shift the weight back on to the right side. At the same time turn the waist to the left, taking the hands up to the side. Left hand facing inwards and right palm facing down.

3) Step back with the left foot, simultaneously sweep the right hand down and across the body. The left hand pushes straight forward. The palm turning to face forward.

1) Sit back on the left. Keep the body facing forward.

2) Turn the waist to the right. Raise the right hand forward and, as it reaches shoulder height, turn the waist to the right taking the hands out to the side.

3) Step back with the right foot, at the same time sweep down with the left hand and push forward with the right, turning the palm forward.

1) Shift the weight back on to the right side.

2) Perform the next two steps as previously described. It is important that the feet are kept parallel throughout the sequence.

3)

Flying Oblique
1) Turn the left hand so that the palm is facing up.

2) Take the right hand up and round, coming to rest with the fingertips touching the left wrist. Palm facing down.

3) Turn the right foot out on the heel. At the same time drop the body down, taking the right hand to just below the left elbow. Turn the waist and look down diagonally to the right.

1) Step straight through with the left foot.

2) Turn the left foot forward on the heel and place it flat on the ground.

3) Shift the weight to the left side. Allow the right foot to turn on the ball of the foot.

Raise Hands and Step Up
1) Step round to the front with the right foot. At the same time the right hand also comes round. The palm faces towards you.

2) Take the left hand down so that both palms are facing each other.

3) Shift the weight forward. The back leg is straight keeping a line from the ground to the top of the head.

1) Step in to shoulder width with the left foot. The angle of the upper body is maintained from the previous posture.

2) Straighten the body, keeping the knees bent.

3) Stand up naturally raising the right palm forward, lowering the left down to the side, palm facing back.

1) White Crane Flaps its Wings
Bend forward from the waist. Allow the left hand to come forward as you bend. Keep the legs straight and do not bend too much.

2) Using the waist, turn the upper body to the left.

3) Raise the left hand in a circular way up and round to the left side of the head.

1) Raise the body up to a standing position, still facing left.

2) Turn the waist so that you are facing the front.

3) Take the hands down with the left hand facing forward. The right hand is facing towards you with the fingers pointing to the left. Keep the elbows down.

Brush Knee Twist Step
1) Sink down, turn on the ball of the right foot so that you are facing to the left. The left hand leads and both hands are on the centre line of the body.

2) Take the hands out to the right, right hand facing in with the fingers pointing forward. The left palm faces down. Simultaneously take a small step out with the left foot.

3) Brush down with the left hand, circling in front of the body, finishing outside the line of the left leg. Let the right palm turn to face forward to complete the movement.

Seven Stars
1) Shift the weight back on to the right side.

2) Drop the elbow allowing the hand to come back towards you.

3) Take the left hand up, touching the right fingers to the wrist.

1) Needle at Sea Bottom
Take the left foot back on the toes.

2) Raise the right hand above the left, fingers pointing forward.

3) Bend down, extending the right hand to the front centre of the body. The left hand comes back towards the right shoulder.

Fan Through The Back
1) Step forward with the left foot. Raise the body slightly.

2) Shift the weight forward raising the right hand, with the left hand placed at the elbow.

3) Turn the left foot on the heel to an angle of 45°. The right hand turns anti-clockwise so that the palm is facing out.

1) Take a step back and round with the right foot.

2) Sit into the stance. The weight is evenly distributed between the feet.

3) Fan the hands, the right hand palm up, above the head. The left palm faces away from you.

Turn the Body & Swing Fist
1) Turn the body round making sure the right foot is parallel with the left. The right hand touches the left with the palm facing the ground.

2) Turn the waist to the left, at the same time the right hand is down in a fist inside the left.

3) Roll the left hand over the right wrist. As you do so allow the right hand to come forward in a back fist, followed by the front palm of the left hand.

1) Step Back, Parry & Punch
Shift the weight back to the left side.

2) Make a complete circle to the right with the hands, also turning the waist. As the hands reach the top of the circle, step back taking the hands to the front centre.

3) Sit back taking the right hand back in a fist to waist.

1) Turn the waist to the right. The left hand comes across the front of the body with the movement of the waist.

2) Turn the waist back to the left, at the same time the left hand comes back palm down to the front centre.

3) Punch through with the right hand, the left fingers touch at the right elbow.

Step Up, Grasping The Bird's Tail
1) Sit back, taking the weight on to the right side. Bring the hands to the centre line of the body, the fingertips touching just below the right hand.

2) Keeping the weight back, take the hands down to the centre, the right palm facing up and the left palm facing down.

3) Shift the weight forward straightening the body. At the same time the hands are brought up to the front centre.

1) Step forward with the right foot.

2) Shift the weight forward turning the waist so that the hands are 45° to the front left corner.

3) Turn the waist taking the hands to the right corner.

1) Sit back allowing the hands to come back to you slightly.

2) Press down to the centre, the right palm turned down.

3) Shift the weight forward pushing forward and diagonally out with the right palm.

Single Whip
1) Turn the right foot forward on the heel, at the same time the right hand turns down bringing the fingertips and thumb together.

2) Take the left foot a small step out to the left touching the toes down. Take care not to step out too far.

2A) Settle the body into the centre of the stance. The weight is equally on both feet.

3) Take the left hand across the front of the body, turning the waist to the left. As you turn the waist forward turn the left hand palm forward. Finally sink a little more into the stance.

Wave Hands in Clouds
1) Turn the right foot on the heel to an angle of 45°, at the same time shift the weight to the right. The right hand is palm down & left hand is palm down.

2) Take the left hand in a curve up and touch the right wrist. Turn the left foot on the heel also to an angle of 45°.

3) Turn the left foot again on the heel out to the left, shifting the weight to the left. Scribe an arc up and out with the left hand.

1) Turn the body to the left diagonally, at the same time the left hand turns out and the right hand comes down to the thigh with the palm facing forward. The right foot follows the movement of the body.

2) Step in with the right foot, the heels are close together.

3) Straighten the posture by pushing the knees slightly forward. At the same time the right hand is brought up in an arc, the fingertips touching the left wrist.

1) Open the stance by turning the right foot out on the heel, simultaneously the right hand moves up and back in an arc.

2) Turn the body to face the front right corner. Allow the left foot to turn on the toes. The right hand turns out while the left comes down to the thigh with the palm facing out.

3) Step back with the left foot, raising the left hand to the right wrist.

1) Shift the weight back on to the left, turning the left foot out as you do so. The left hand arcs up and back.

2) Turn to the left taking the right hand down to the thigh and the left hand is lowered, palm turned out. The right foot follows the movement of the body.

3) Step in with the right foot. This is followed in one movement of straightening the posture and raising the right hand to the left wrist.

1) Open the posture by turning the right foot out on the heel, at the same time the right hand arcs up and back.

2) Turn the body to face the front right corner. Allow the left foot to turn on the toes. The right hand turns out while the left comes down to the thigh, the palm facing out.

3) Step back with the left foot, at the same time the left hand is raised to touch the right wrist.

Single Whip
1) Turn the right foot forward on the heel, at the same time the right hand turns down bringing the fingertips and thumb together.

2) Take the left foot a small step out to the left touching the toes down. Take care not to step out too far.

2A) Settle the body into the centre of the stance. The weight is equally on both feet.

3) Take the left hand across the front of the body, turning the waist to the left. As you turn the waist forward, turn the left hand palm forward. Finally sink a little more into the stance.

High Pat The Horse
1) Turn the body to the left by pivoting on the right heel. The left hand is lowered to the side, palm facing up. The right hand is slightly raised, palm down.

2) Draw the left foot back on the toes.

3) Sink down, drop the right hand down so that the left fingers touch the wrist.

1) Step forward with the left foot.

Turn the Body To Face Left
2) Shift the weight forward taking the hands back towards your body. The right hand above, facing down. The left hand below and facing up.

3) Turn the waist to the right and continuing until you face the front. The hands are extended as the waist turns, eventually coming to rest at 45° in front of the body.

1) Turn the left foot to an angle of 45°, at the same time the right hand comes round and crosses the left wrist, making fists with both hands. The right fist turns inwards and the left fist faces out.

2) Bring the right foot to the front of the stance by scribing an arc. The knee slightly turned inwards.

3) Remaining at the same height, straighten the posture.

Raise The Right Leg and Kick Out in a Curve.
1) Raise the right leg, keeping the toes pointing down.

2) Turn the hands down and open them. The left hand on top, the right underneath. Both palms face down. Then separate them to approximately shoulder width.

3) Allow the kick to unfold as you turn the waist to the right corner. At the same time the hands fan out. It is important that the right hand is directly in line with the right leg.

High Pat The Horse
1) Turn the body to the left and lower the right foot.

Turn Body to Face Right.
2) Shift forward, left hand down palm out and, as it reaches the right hand, both hands then come towards the body. Left hand on top, palm down, right hand underneath, palm up.

3) Turn the waist to the left allowing the hands to extend and separate as you turn the waist forward. The right palm is facing up, the left facing down.

1) Turn the right foot out on the heel, at the same time the left hand comes round to the outside. Make fists with both hands, crossing them at the wrists, left fist facing in, right fist facing out.

2) Bring the left foot round in an arc to the front of the stance. The knee is slightly turned inwards.

3) Keep the same height of stance and straighten the posture.

Raise the Leg and Kick Out in a Curve
1) Raise the left leg keeping the toes pointing down.

2) Open the hands, palms down, the left placed under the right. Separate them to almost shoulder width.

3) Turn the waist to the left, allowing the left foot to kick in a curve, at the same time fan the hands out, the left directly over the kicking leg.

Turn Around And Kick with The Heel
1) Take the left foot down behind the right.

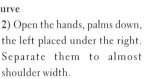

2) Turn round on the right heel. Use the left foot to maintain the balance.

3) Raise the left knee and kick forward with the heel. At the same time the left hand arcs forward and the right hand is taken out to the side.

Brush Knee & Twist Step
1) Lower the left foot down.

2) Turn the waist to the right. The left hand is taken to the right, palm facing down, and the right palm faces inwards.

3) Shift the weight on to the left foot, at the same time brush down and across with the left hand and push forward with the right.

1) Step forward with the right foot.

2) Turn the waist to the left taking the hands up and to the side. The right palm is down and the left is facing inwards.

3) Shift the weight to the right foot. Brush down and across with the right hand at the same time pushing forward with the left.

Step Forward & Punch Down
1) Step forward with the left foot.

2) Turn the waist to the right taking the hands up and to the right.

2A) Brush down with the left hand, at the same time drop the foot on to the ground. The left hand is palm out.

3) Shifting the weight forward keep circling the left hand until it comes across the body. Punch down to complete the posture. The left fingers touch the right elbow just below the bicep.

Turn Body and Swing Fist
1) Turn the left foot to point to the right, on the heel. At the same time fold the right arm over the left.

2) Turn the body 180° and take a step out to the right. This is to maintain shoulder width with the feet.

3) Shift the weight forward taking the right hand forward in a back fist. This is followed by the left palm.

Step Up to High Pat The Horse
1) Step forward with the left foot. At the same time turn the hands anti-clockwise, opening both and pushing the right forward.

Turn Body to Face The Left.
2) Shift the weight forward taking the hands back towards the body. The right hand is above, palm down, the left palm up. Keep the hands 6" apart.

3) Turn the waist to the right allowing the hands to extend out and opening as the body turns forward.

1) Turn the left foot on the heel taking the right hand round and outside the left. Close the hands into fists and cross them at the wrists.

2) Take the right foot in an arc and place it in front of the stance, the knee turned slightly inwards.

3) Straighten the posture.

Raise the Right Leg and Kick Out in A Curve
1) Raise the right leg, keeping the toes pointing down.

2) Turn the hands down and open them. The left hand on top, the right underneath. Both palms face down. Then separate them to approximately shoulder width.

3) Allow the kick to unfold as you turn the waist to the right corner. At the same time the hands fan out. It is important that the right hand is directly in line with the right leg.

Step Back To Seven Stars
1) Take the right foot back in a straight line.

Turn Body to Face Right.
2) Sit back on the right side, at the same time bend the right elbow slightly.

3) Place the left hand on top of the right.

Step Back To Strike The Tiger
1) Step back with the left foot. At the same time extend the right hand, taking the left hand to the right elbow.

2) Turn the left foot until it is straight. shift the weight on to the left simultaneously press down with both hands facing down.

3) Turn the waist, at the same time circle the left hand up to the head and the right hand turning inwards. Allow the right foot to turn with the whole body.

3A) *(Reverse Angle)*

Twist The Body and Kick
1) Turn the left foot to right, on the heel. The waist turns to the right, whilst the right foot comes in. The right hand circles above the head and the left hand comes across to the right shoulder.

2) Circle the left hand down and up above the head in a fist. The right hand circles down in front of the body, also in a fist. Both palms face upwards.

3) Open the hands and cross them, the left over the right. Separate them and kick out diagonally with the sole of the right foot.

Boxing The Ears
1) Place the right foot in front of the body, on the heel. At the same time take the hands palms out straight to the front, shoulder width apart.

2) Move the weight forward on to the right foot, moving the hands down to the side of the body. Keep the palms down.

3) Making fists with both hands, then circle them up. The fists at this point are kept about eight inches apart.

1) Turn the right foot out on the heel, at the same time the left hand comes round to the outside. Make fists with both hands, crossing them at the wrists, left fist facing in, right fist facing out.

2) Bring the left foot round in an arc to the front of the stance. The knee is slightly turned inwards.

3) Keep the same height of stance and straighten the posture.

Raise The Left Leg and Kick Out In A Curve.
1) Raise the left leg keeping the toes pointing down.

2) Open the hands, palm down, the left placed under the right. Separate them to almost shoulder width.

3) Turn the waist to the left, allowing the left foot to kick in a curve. At the same time fan the hands out, the left directly over the kicking leg.

Turn Around And Kick Heel
1) Take the left leg to the right crossing it over the right leg. Cross the hands in fists. Look over the left shoulder. Weight on left foot, right heel off ground.

2) Turn around 180° on the left heel. Do not take the left foot too far round. Keep it pointing out to the left.

3) Raise the right leg and kick with the sole, fanning the hands out at the same time. The left arm out to the side, the right, directly over the the kicking leg.

Swing The Fist
1) Place the right foot down in front of the stance.

2) Take the right hand inside the left by turning the waist. Make fists with both hands.

3) Take the right hand up and forward in a back fist, followed by the palm of the left. Allow the left foot to turn forward on the heel to finish the posture.

Step Up Parry and Punch
1) Step forward with the left foot.

2) Place the fist in the right palm, circling the hands down to the right. Turning the waist circle the hands up, as they reach the top of the circle, shift the weight forward.

3) Sit back taking the right fist to the side.

1) Turn the waist to the right, taking the left hand across the body.

2) Turning the waist to the left, the left hand comes back to the centre, palm down.

3) Punch forward taking the left hand to rest at the right elbow.

As If Shutting A Door
1) Place the left hand, palm up, under the forearm.

2) Shift the weight back. Take both hands up and back so that both palms are facing you.

3) Shift the weight forward, turning the hands so that the palms are facing away from you.

Embrace Tiger and Return To Mountain
1) Move the weight back slightly, at the same time turn the left foot on the heel and drop the hands straight down. Shift the weight back on to the left side.

2) Turn the body to face 45° to the right rear. As you turn also turn the hands so that the palms are facing out. The heel of the right foot touches the ground.

3) Take the weight on to the right side, at the same time the right hand comes up and the left hand is down to the left and both palms are facing forward.

Cross Hands
1) Step in with the left foot making sure that you maintain a shoulder width stance.

2) Turn the right foot from the heel to face forward, at the same time cross the hands in front, right hand on the outside.

3) Stand up straight.

Oblique Brush Knee Twist Step
1) Sink down.

2) Take a step diagonally to the left, at the same time turn the waist taking the hands out to the right.

3) Repeat previous style allowing the right foot to turn forward on the heel so that the whole body is focussed in one direction.

Turn Body Brush Knee Twist Step
1) Turn the left foot on the heel, at the same time the left hand comes up and round so that both palms are facing each other.

2) Keep both hands out to the left as you turn 180⁰ to the opposite angle and step out to the right.

3) Repeat previous style. Again the foot turns on the heel to point in the direction of the focus.

Seven Stars
1) Shift the weight back to the left side.

2) Bend the left arm bringing the hand slightly towards you.

36

3) Place the right hand on top of the left.

Grasping the Bird's Tail
1) Turn the hands so that the right hand is palm up and the left is palm down. At the same time bend forward taking the hands down in front of the body.

2) Shift the weight forward turning the waist and taking the hands out diagonally to the left. The right knee does not extend beyond the toes.

3) Remain in the same stance and turn the waist diagonally to the right.

1) Shift the weight back to the left taking the hands back slightly towards you.

2) Turn the hands so that the right hand is facing down and the left is facing up. Again take the hands down to the centre of the body.

3) Move forward so that the weight is on the right side. Take the hands up and out diagonally left. The left hand is palm up and the right is palm down.

Oblique Single Whip
1) Turn the right foot forward on the heel, at the same time the right hand turns down bringing the fingertips and thumb together.

2) Take the left foot a small step out to the left touching the toes down. Take care not to step out too far.

2A) Settle the body into the centre of the stance. The weight is equally on both feet.

3) Take the left hand across the front of the body, turning the waist to the left. As you turn the waist forward turn the left hand, palm forward. Finally sink a little more into the stance.

Steven Stars
1) Turning on the left heel shift the weight to the left side, turning the body to square up the stance.

2) Step in with the right foot, at the same time take the left hand into the centre.

3) Place the right hand on top of the left. the left fingers touching the right wrist.

Parting The Wild Horse's Mane
1) Take the right hand down and across the body. The left hand moves to the right shoulder. Turn the waist to the left. Remember this is one movement.

2) Step out with the right foot and shift the weight forward, turning the waist so that the body faces the front.

3) Turn the waist to the left, taking the hands out to the left. Allow the hands to pass each other. This keeps the arms at a natural length.

3A) Continue turning the waist and separating the arms. The arms should be at 45° from the body. The right hand is palm up, the left is facing down.

Seven Stars
1) Again, sit back on the left side.

2) Drop the left hand to the centre stepping in with the right foot.

3) Place the right hand on top of the left, left fingers touching the right wrist.

Parting The Wild Horse's Mane
1) Take the right hand down and across the body. the left hand moves to the right shoulder.

2) Step out with the right foot and shift the weight forward, turning the waist so that the body faces the front.

3) Turn the waist to the left taking the hands up and out, allowing the palms to pass each other. Continue turning the waist and separating the arms.

1) Turn the right foot out on the heel, at the same time the right hand comes across to the left shoulder.

2) Take the left hand down and across the body.

3) Step forward with the left foot.

1) Take the weight forward on to the left foot. Keep the body facing forward.

2) Turn the waist to the right.

3) Turn the waist back round to the front, separating the hands. The left hand is palm up and the right is palm down.

1) Turn the left foot out on the heel, at the same time the left hand moves to the right shoulder.

2) Take the right hand down and across the body.

3) Step through with the right foot.

1) Move the weight on to the right side.

2) Turn the waist to the left.

3) Complete the posture by turning the waist forward. the hands move out and up, coming round to the front.

Seven Stars
1) Again, sit back on the left side.

2) Drop the left hand to the centre stepping in with the right foot.

3) Place the right hand on top of the left, left fingers touching the right wrist.

Parting The Wild Horse's Mane
1) Take the right hand down and across the body. The left hand moves to the right shoulder. Turn the waist to the left. Remember this is one movement.

2) Step out with the right foot and shift the weight forward, turning the waist so that the body faces the front.

3) Turn the waist to the left, taking the hands out to the left. Allow the hands to pass each other. This keep the arms at a natural length.

1) Turn the right foot out on the heel, at the same time the right hand comes across to the left shoulder.

2) Take the left hand down and across the body.

3) Step forward with the left foot.

Fair Lady Weaves at Shuttle
1) Take the weight forward, at the same time the left hand circles forward palm up at an angle of 45°. The right hand is at the left elbow, palm down.

2) Sit back on the right side taking the left hand back towards you.

2A) Continue by turning the waist to the right. Be careful not to overturn the waist.

3) Turn the waist to the left, push out to the front left corner by turning the left hand up and out. The right hand also pushes out.

1) Turn the left foot to the right on the heel. The right hand comes down across the body, palm up. The left goes across to the right shoulder, palm down.

2) Turn 180° and step out with the right foot.

3) Shift the weight forward on to the right side. The right hand circles out, palm up, to an angle of 45°. The left hand is at the right elbow, palm down.

1) Sit back taking the right hand back slightly towards you.

2) Turn the waist to the left.

3) Shift the weight forward, turning the waist whilst pushing out with both palms to the right front corner.

Seven Stars
1) Shift the weight back to the left side.

2) Step in with the right foot, at the same time the left hand comes to the centre of the body.

3) Place the right hand on top of the left fingers.

Parting The Wild Horse's Mane
1) Take the right hand down and across the body. The left hand moves to the right shoulder.

2) Step out with the right foot and shift the weight forward.

3) Turn the waist to the left taking the hands up and out. Continue turning the waist and separating the hands. The right hand is palm up, the left, palm down.

1) Turn the right foot out on the heel. Take the right hand across to the left shoulder.

2) Drop the left hand down and across the body.

3) Step through with the left foot.

1) Turn the waist to the left, taking the weight forward. Extend the left hand to the left corner. The right hand is at the left elbow, palm down.

2) Sit back and turn the waist to the right.

3) Complete the form by shifting the weight to the left side, turning the waist to the left. Both palms face out as you push to the corner.

1) Turn the left foot on the heel to the right. The left hand comes to the right shoulder, palm down. The right hand is placed across the body, palm up.

2) Turn 180° to the right and step out with the right foot.

3) Shift the weight forward extending the right hand to the right corner. The left hand is placed at the elbow, palm down.

1) Sit back, bending the right elbow, taking the right hand slightly towards you.

2) Turn the waist to the left.

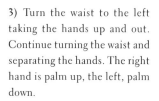

3) Shift the weight forward turning the waist to the right. Both palms face out as you push to the right corner.

Seven Stars
1) Shift the weight back to the left side.

2) Turn the waist to the left taking the left hand to the centre.

3) Place the right hand on top of the left.

Grasping the Bird's Tail.
1) Turn the hands so that the right hand is palm up and the left is palm down. At the same time bend forward taking the hands down in front of the body.

2) Shift the weight forward turning the waist and taking the hands out diagonally to the left. The right knee does not extend beyond the toes.

3) Remain in the same stance and turn the waist diagonally to the right.

1) Shift the weight back to the left taking the hands back slightly towards you.

2) Turn the hands so that the right hand is facing down and the left is facing up. Again take the hands down to the centre of the body.

3) Move forward so that the weight is on the right side. Take the hands up and out diagonally left. The left hand is palm up and the right is palm down.

Single Whip
1) Turn the right foot forward on the heel, at the same time the right hand turns down bringing the fingertips and thumb together.

2) Take the left foot a small step out to the left touching the toes down. Take care not to step out too far.

2A) Settle the body into the centre of the stance. The weight is equally on both feet.

3) Take the left hand across the front of the body, turning the waist to the left. As you turn the waist forward turn the left hand, palm forward. Finally sink a little more into the stance.

Wave Hands In Clouds
1) Turn the right foot on the heel to an angle of 45⁰, at the same time shift the weight to the right. The right hand is palm down and left hand is palm down.

2) Take the left hand in a curve up and touch the right wrist. Turn the left foot on the heel also to an angle of 45⁰.

3) Turn the left foot again on the heel out to the left, shifting the weight to the left. Scribe an arc up and out with the left hand.

1) Turn the body to the left diagonally, at the same time the left hand turns out and the right hand comes down to the thigh with the palm facing forward. The right foot follows the movement of the body.

2) Step in with the right foot. The heels are close together.

3) Straighten the posture by pushing the knees slightly forward, at the same time the right hand is brought up in an arc, the fingertips touching the left wrist.

1) Open the stance by turning the right foot out on the heel, simultaneously the right hand moves up and back in an arc.

2) Turn the body to face the front right corner. Allow the left foot to turn on the toes. The right hand turns out while the left comes down to the thigh with the palms facing out.

3) Step back with the left foot, raising the left hand to the right wrist.

1) Shift the weight back on to the left, turning the left foot out as you do so. The left hand arcs up and back.

2) Turn to the left taking the right hand down to the thigh and the left hand is lowered, palm turned out. The right foot follows the movement of the body.

3) Step in with the right foot. This is followed in one movement of straightening the posture and raising the right hand to the left wrist.

1) Open the posture by turning the right foot out on the heel, at the same time the right hand arcs up and back.

2) Turn the body to face the front right corner. Allow the left foot to turn on the toes. The right hand turns out while the left comes down to the thigh, the palm facing out.

3) Step back with the left foot, at the same time the left hand is raised to touch the right wrist.

Single Whip
1) Turn the right foot forward on the heel, at the same time the right hand turns down bringing the fingertips and thumb together.

2) Take the left foot a small step out to the left touching the toes down. Take care not to step out too far.

2A) Settle the body into the centre of the stance. The weight is equally on both feet.

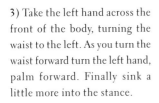

3) Take the left hand across the front of the body, turning the waist to the left. As you turn the waist forward turn the left hand, palm forward. Finally sink a little more into the stance.

Snake Creeps Down
1) Turn the left foot out on the heel, at the same time take the weight to the left and extend the left hand.

2) Turn the right foot forward on the ball of the foot, extending the right arm simultaneously. The left hand comes back towards the chest.

3) Turn the right foot on the heel to face out to an angle of 45°.

1) Take the weight back to the right foot, keeping the knee in line with the foot. The hands come back towards the body.

2) Turn the waist to the right, circling the hands with the waist. When the hands are over the right leg turn the waist to the left & drop to the lower stance.

3) Follow the direction the hands are pointing, come through the posture. This takes the weight naturally on to the left side. The left hand rises above the head, palm facing out.

Golden Cockerel Stands on One Leg

1) Bring the right foot through bending the knee and turning the sole to face inwards. Reverse the hand positions.

2) Place the right foot down. The right hand comes down to the centre, palm up. The left hand comes up to the inside of the elbow, palm up.

3) Shift the weight forward extending the left hand and withdraw the right hand to the elbow.

1) Kick straight through with the left foot, toes pointing forward.

Step Back & Repulse The Monkey

2) Turn the waist to the left taking the hands up to the side. Left hand faces in, right faces down. Withdraw left foot, opening knee out, sole inwards.

3) Step back with the left foot and complete the style.

1) Sit back on the left. Keep the body facing forward.

2) Turn the waist to the right. Raise the right hand forward and, as it reaches shoulder height, turn the waist to the right taking the hands out to the side.

3) Step back with the right foot, at the same time sweep down with the left hand and push forward with the right, turning the palm forward.

1) Shift the weight back on to the right side.	2) Perform the next two steps as previously described. It is important that the feet are kept parallel throughout the sequence.	3)	**Step Aside Flying Oblique** 1) Turn the left hand so that the palm is facing up.

2) Take the right hand up and round, coming to rest with the fingertips touching the left wrist. Palm facing down.	3) Turn the right foot out on the heel. At the same time drop the body down, taking the right hand to just below the left elbow. Turn the waist and look down diagonally to the right.	1) Step straight through with the left foot.	2) Step back with the left foot, angling the body forward.

3) Shift the weight back and extend the left hand up, the right hand moves forward.	**Raise Hands and Step Up** 1) Move the weight to the right, at the same time the right hand turns in as the left comes down. Both palms face each other. Turn the left foot forward on the heel.	2) Step in with the left foot and straighten the posture.	3) Stand up raising the right palm out, lowering the left palm, facing down.

White Crane Flaps its Wings
1) Bend forward from the waist. Allow the left hand to come forward as you bend. Keep the legs straight and do not bend too much.

2) Using the waist, turn the upper body to the left.

3) Raise the left hand in a circular way up and round to the side of the head.

1) Raise the body up to a standing position, still facing left.

2) Turn the waist so that you are facing the front.

3) Take the hands down with the left hand facing forward. The right hand is facing towards you with the fingers pointing to the left. Keep the elbows down.

Seven Stars Brush Knee Twist Step
1) Sink down, turn on the ball of the right foot so that you are facing to the left. The left hand leads and both hands are on the centre line of the body.

2) Take the hands out to the right, right hand facing in with the fingers pointing forward. The left palm faces down. Simultaneously take a small step out with the left foot.

3) Brush down with the left hand, circling in front of the body, finishing outside the line of the left leg. Let the right palm turn to face forward to complete the movement.

Seven Stars
1) Sit back on the right side

2) Bend the right elbow.

3) Place the left hand on top of the right.

Needle at Sea Bottom
1) Take the left foot back on the toes.

2) Raise the right hand above the left, fingers pointing forward.

3) Bend down, extending the right hand to the front centre of the body. The left hand comes back towards the right shoulder.

Fan Through The Back
1) Step forward with the left foot. Raise the body slightly.

2) Shift the weight forward raising the right hand, with the left hand placed at the elbow.

3) Turn the left foot on the heel to an angle of 45⁰. The right hand turns anti-clockwise so that the palm is facing out.

1) Take a step back and round with the right foot.

2) Sit into the stance. The weight is evenly distributed between the feet.

3) Fan the hands, the right hand palm up, above the head. The left palm faces away from you.

Turn Body and Swing Fist
1) Turn the body round making sure the right foot is parallel with the left. The right hand touches the left with the palm facing the ground.

2) Turn the waist to the left, at the same time the right hand is down in a fist inside the left.

3) Roll the left hand over the right wrist. As you do so allow the right hand to come forward in a back fist, followed by the front palm of the left hand.

Step up Parry and Punch
1) Step forward with left foot.

2) Make a gentle fist with the right hand and touch it to the left palm. Turn the waist to the right. Circle the hands up, as they reach the top of the circle, shift the weight forward.

3) Sit back taking the right hand back in a fist to the waist.

1) Turn the waist to the right. The left hand comes across the front of the body with the movement of the waist.

2) Turn the waist back to the left. At the same time the left hand comes back palm down to the front centre.

3) Punch through with the right hand. The left fingers touch at the right elbow.

Step up Grasping The Bird's Tail
1) Sit back taking the weight on to the right side. Bring the hands to the centre line of the body, the fingertips touching just below the right hand.

2) Keeping the weight back, take the hand down to the centre, the right palm facing up and the left palm facing down.

3) Shift the weight forward straightening the body. At the same time the hands are brought up to the front centre.

1) Step forward with the right foot.

2) Shift the weight forward turning the waist so that the hands are 45⁰ to the front left corner.

3) Turn the waist taking the hands to the right corner.

1) Sit back allowing the hands to come back to you slightly.

2) Press down to the centre, the right palm turned down.

3) Shift the weight forward pushing forward and diagonally out with the right palm.

Single Whip
1) Turn the right foot forward on the heel, at the same time the right hand turns down bringing the fingertips and thumb together.

2) Take the left foot a small step out to the left touching the toes down. Take care not to step out too far.

2A) Settle the body into the centre of the stance. The weight is equally on both feet.

3) Take the left hand across the front of the body, turning the waist to the left. As you turn the waist forward turn the left hand, palm forward. Finally sink a little more into the stance.

Wave Hands In Clouds
1) Turn the right foot on the heel to an angle of 45⁰, at the same time shift the weight to the right. The right hand is palm down and left hand is palm down.

2) Take the left hand in a curve up and touch the right wrist. Turn the left foot on the heel also to an angle of 45⁰.

3) Turn the left foot again on the heel out to the left, shifting the weight to the left. Scribe an arc up and out with the left hand.

1) Turn the body to the left diagonally, at the same time the left hand turns out and the right hand comes down to the thigh with the palm facing forward. The right foot follows the movement of the body.

2) Step in with the right foot, the heels are close together.

3) Straighten the posture by pushing the knees slightly forward, at the same time the right hand is brought up in an arc, the fingertips touching the left wrist.

1) Open the stance by turning the right foot out on the heel, simultaneously the right hand moves up and back in an arc.

2) Turn the body to face the front right corner. Allow the left foot to turn on the toes. The right hand turns out while the left comes down to the thigh with the palm facing out.

3) Step back with the left foot, raising the left hand to the right wrist.

1) Shift the weight back on to the left, turning the left foot out as you do so. The left hand arcs up and back.

2) Turn to the left taking the right hand down to the thigh and the left hand is lowered palm turned out. The right foot follows the movement of the body

3) Step in with the right foot. This is followed in one movement of straightening the posture and raising the right hand to the left wrist.

1) Open the posture by turning the right foot out on the heel, at the same time the right hand arcs up and back.

2) Turn the body to face the front right corner. Allow the left foot to turn on the toes. The right hand turns out while the left comes down to the thigh, the palm facing out.

3) Step back with the left foot, at the same time the left hand is raised to touch the right wrist.

Single Whip
1) Turn the right foot forward on the heel, at the same time the right hand turns down bringing the fingertips and thumb together.

2) Take the left foot a small step out to the left touching the toes down. Take care not to step out too far.

2A) Settle the body into the centre of the stance. The weight is equally on both feet.

3) Take the left hand across the front to the body, turning the waist to the left. As you turn the waist forward turn the left hand, palm forward. Finally sink a little more into the stance.

High Pat The Horse
1) Turn the body to the left by pivoting on the right heel. The left hand is lowered to the side, palm facing up. The right hand is slightly raised, palm down.

2) Draw the left foot back on the toes.

3) Sink down, drop the right hand down so that the left fingers touch the wrist.

Slap The Face
1) Step forward with the left foot

2) Turn the waist to the left, taking the left hand up to the side, palm forward. the right hand is just under the elbow, palm down.

3) Take the weight forward, at the same time the left hand is extended forward.

Cross Hands and Single Hand Sweep Lotus Leg
1) Turn the left foot on the heel to point out to the left completing 180° turn. The left hand comes all the way across the body.

2) Raise the right foot up to the left.

3) Take the right foot in an arc. The foot and hand meet in the centre of the body.

Brush Knee Twist Step
1) Place the right foot on the ground.

2) Turn the waist to the left, taking the hands up to the left.

3) Sweep down and across with the right hand. The left moves straight forward, turning the palm forward.

Step Up To Punch The Groin
1) Take a step forward with the left foot.

2) Turn the waist to the right, taking the hands up to the right.

3) Take the left hand down, palm out. At the same time place the left foot on the ground. Start to circle the right hand up and back.

3A) Continue to circle the left hand up and back towards you. The right hand is simultaneously circling out the back, down and punching up in a curve.

Step Up Grasping The Bird's Tail
1) Sit back taking the weight on to the right side. Bring the hands to the centre line of the body, the fingertips touching just below the right hand.

2) Keeping the weight back, take the hands down to the centre, the right palm facing up and the left palm facing down.

3) Shift the weight forward straightening the body. At the same time the hands are brought up to the front centre.

1) Step forward with the right foot.

2) Shift the weight forward turning the waist so that the hands are 45° to the front left corner.

3) Turn the waist taking the hands to the right corner.

1) Sit back allowing the hands to come back to you slightly.

2) Press down to the centre, the right palm turned down.

3) Shift the weight forward pushing forward and diagonally out with the right palm.

Single Whip
1) Turn the right foot forward on the heel, at the same time the right hand turns down bringing the fingertips and thumb together.

2) Take the left foot a small step out to the left touching the toes down. Take care not to step out too far.

2A) Settle the body into the centre of the stance. The weight is equally on both feet.

3) Take the left hand across the front of the body, turning the waist to the left. As you turn the waist forward turn the left hand, palm forward. Finally sink a little more into the stance.

Snake Creeps Down
1) Turn the left foot out on the heel, at the same time take the weight to the left and extend the left hand.

2) Turn the right foot forward on the ball of the foot, extending the right arm simultaneously. The left hand comes back towards the chest.

3) Turn the right foot on the heel to face out to an angle of 45⁰.

1) Take the weight back to the right foot, keeping the knee in line with the foot. The hands come back towards the body.

2) Turn the waist to the right, circling the hands with the waist. When the hands are over the right leg turn the waist to the left and drop to the lower stance.

3) Follow the direction the hands are pointing, come through the posture. This takes the weight naturally on to the left side. The left hand rises above the head, palm facing out.

Step Up Seven Stars
1) Step forward with the right foot. Place the toes on the ground. The hands cross in front of the body, left hand on top.

Step Back To Ride The Tiger
2) Step back with the right foot.

3) Shift the weight back to the right side. Take the hands back towards you as you move.

1) Take the left foot back on the toes.

2) Circle the hands down and up to shoulder height. The right palm faces out. The left fingertips and thumb come together.

3) Circle the left hand up and over, taking it out behind you as you pivot on the toes of the right foot. Meanwhile, the right hand moves above the head. palm out. Upper body inclines forward.

1) Kick straight ahead with the left foot.

Turn The Body & Slap The Face
2) Pivot round on the ball of the right foot. The left hand comes up in a circle so the palm faces forward. The right hand comes across the front of the body, palm down.

3) Place the left foot down and take the weight forward. The left hand comes forward to complete the movement.

Turn The Body and Double Hand Sweep The Lotus Leg
1) Turn on the left heel, taking the hands round and out to the right. The body faces the rear corner.

2) Sweep the right foot clockwise in a circle, up and in front of the body. The hands sweep across to the left and brush the foot as it reaches the top of the circle.

3) Place the right foot down to a point 45⁰ to the left. Both palms are extended, the body is also turned to face 45°.

Draw The Bow To Shoot The Tiger
1) Turn the right foot on the heel to point to the right. Shift the weight back and press down with both hands.

2) Turn the waist to the right until both hands are at the right side, fingers pointing down. The left foot comes round with the waist movement.

3) Take the hands up to the rear, palms facing down.

1) Make fists with both hands.

2) Turn the waist to the left allowing the hands to come forward. The right thumb is pointing down.

3) Take both hands forward. Maintain a circular shape with the arms.

High Pat The Horse
1) Step forward with the left foot. Open both hands and take the right hand forward. The left hand is palm up and touching the right wrist.

Slap The Face
2) Turn the waist to the left taking the left hand up to the side, palm forward. The right hand is palm down below the left elbow.

3) Take the weight forward, extending the left palm forward.

Turn The Body & Swing Fist
1) Take the left hand down and under the right arm. turn the left foot on the heel to point to the right.

2) Turn round 180° and step out to the right.

3) Shift the weight forward taking the right hand in a back fist followed by the left palm.

Step Up To High Pat The Horse
1) Step forward with the left foot. Turn the hands over, anticlockwise taking the right palm forward. The left hand touches the right wrist.

Step Up Grasping The Bird's Tail
2) Turn the waist to the right taking the hands out to the right.

2A) Turning the waist to the left in a continuous movement turn in the hands so that the right hand is palm up and the left is palm down.

2B) As the hands pass the chest step forward with the right foot, taking the hands out to the front left corner.

3) Turn the waist to the right, taking the hands to the right corner.

1) Sit back, the hands coming slightly back to you.

2) Turn the right hand down and press into the centre. the left hand is palm up.

3) Take the weight forward and turn the waist to the front left corner. The right hand is palm out, the left is touching the right wrist.

Single Whip
1) Turn the right foot forward on the heel, at the same time the right hand turns down bringing the fingertips and thumb together.

2) Take the left foot a small step out to the left touching the toes down. Take care not to step out too far.

2A) Settle the body into the centre of the stance. The weight is equally on both feet.

3) Take the left hand across the front of the body, turning the waist to the left. As you turn the waist forward, turn the left hand, palm forward. Finally sink a little more into the stance.

Tai Chi At Rest
1) Take the weight on to the right foot. Both palms are facing down.

2) Step in with the left foot. As you cross the hands in front, straighten the right foot. The left hand is above the right, both palms face down.

Completion Style
3) Take the hands out and down in a circular motion. As you lower the hands, stand up to complete the movement.

The Thirteen Tactics
of Tai Chi Chuan

The five steps and the eight powers make the thirteen tactics of Tai Chi.

Each of the steps correspond to one of the five elements.

> Metal is a forward step
> Wood is a backward step
> Water is a step to the left
> Fire is a step to the right
> Earth is central equilibrium

Water and fire will always overcome metal, by rusting or melting, so the tactics against a straight attack (metal) would be either water (step left) or fire (step right). Metal against metal goes against the principle of Tai Chi as it is then a trial of strength. A simple swing of the upper body to the left or right is also making use of the five elements. The interaction between the five elements is endless.

The eight fundamental powers of Tai Chi are:-

Peng
This is an upward movement, whether it be diverting, punching kicking etc.
Lu
Lu is used to divert a straight attack to the side, therefore neutralising.
Qi
Qi is a forward push.
An
Any downward force is An. Such as a push or stamping with the foot.
Cai.
This is an uprooting technique. When an opponent's balance is lost you can destroy it completely by using this style.
Lai
Spiralling an opponent's force back to him is the function of this style.
Zhou
Although technically the use of the elbow, any part of the arm, from the forearm to the elbow is seen as Zhou.
Kao
Striking with the shoulder. This can be used when being pulled forward or striking someone who is holding you from behind, as in Flying Oblique.

All of the above are used in combination and become one technique. They musn't be seen in isolation from one another. In this way they are able to deal with any situation that may occur.

PUSHING HANDS

The Pushing Hands exercise is the first step on the way to understanding the Tai Chi principle, in the martial context. Each style has a specific function, or functions depending on how far one sees into the possibilities of each exercise.

The initial aim of pushing hands is to develop sensitivity. This means using your hands to feel and sense the movement of your partner. It is essential to maintain contact with your partner throughout. This touching is called 'listening' and, with practice, this aspect can be developed to a high degree, so that the slightest movement or intention of your partner can be felt. Keeping in contact with your partner is called 'adhering.' Using both these techniques you can not only sense movement, but you can follow as well, becoming one with your partner.

The styles of pushing hands vary from single handed to double handed, from static to stepping and ranging from specific patterns to free pushing. Apart from developing sensitivity, pushing hands gives a sense of the distance required to make the next step, which is the practice of the practical applications.

Yielding is the technique of soft overcoming the hard. This is one of the main principles of Tai Chi Chuan. Only through the practice of pushing hands will this be understood. When yielding to an oncoming force, it is by coordinating the hands and the waist that you neutralise and redirect this force into the void. The hands are used to detect the direction of the force and the waist, to turn it aside.

In the normal practice of pushing hands, it is a mutual exercise, so that one can develop the techniques of sensing, adhering, neutralising and diverting. Only when it is done freestyle does it change into a contest of skill. It still isn't a contest in the true sense, rather it is a method where one not only puts into practice all the principles of pushing hands, but also takes them into a more realistic situation. Being pushed or thrown, in practice, is an opportunity to strengthen the weaker areas of one's technique.

You should be careful when practicing, to make sure that the principles of Tai Chi are adhered to. No hard strength should be used in any part of pushing hands. Resorting to the use of strength is the easy option. Developing technique is much more difficult. You should question why you were pushed and also, when you push, was it good Tai Chi?

SOLO PUSHING HANDS EXERCISE

Four Directions

Photographs 1 - 4.

1) Starting with the weight on the right side and the waist turned to the left, the left hand is palm up while the right hand is palm down, and held near the elbow.

2) Keeping the weight back, on the right, turn the waist to the right, turning the hands over as you do so.

3) Take the weight forward on to the left foot, at the same time push the right hand forward, while the left remains close to the elbow.

4) The weight remains on the front foot as you push the left hand forward. At the same time withdraw the right hand back towards the elbow.

PARTNER PUSHING HANDS EXERCISE

Four Directions

Photographs 1 - 4.

1) As your partner pushes forward, attach the back of your left hand on to the back of his left wrist. As his push comes through, touch his elbow with the palm of your right hand. The hand movements must be coordinated with the turning of the waist.

2) When your partner pushes with his right hand, reverse the previous posture by turning to the right, adhering to the back of his right wrist with the back of your right hand while your left palm is placed gently on his elbow.

3 - 4) As you push forward, your partner shifts his weight back and adheres to your arm in the same way as previously described in photographs 1 & 2.

This exercise is repeated by continuing the cycle of movements and can be varied by changing which foot is forward and which hand you lead with.

You will see that the person in the dark suit is doing the same sequence of movements as in the solo exercise, whilst the person in the white is doing the reverse.

Four Directions
(*circular*)

This method of pushing hands is the circular variation of the Four Directions style.

1) When you receive the first push you deflect it upwards with the left palm down on the elbow and the back of the right hand placed on the wrist.

2) Following on from this you keep the waist turning to the right, at the same time the right hand is turning so that the palm is then touching the wrist.

3) Your partner then follows with his second push, which is received by meeting it with the left palm on the wrist. As it comes through, continue turning the waist to the left and simultaneously place the right palm on his elbow. This has the effect of pressing down, and taking his push out to the side.

4 - 6) You then push forward with both hands, your partner deflects your push upwards and the sequence is the same as previously described.

Remember that it is a continuous movement and it is important that you keep the flow moving in a calm and relaxed manner. With prolonged practice there develops a strong circular movement that is generated from a very active waist movement.

SEVEN STARS STYLE
Solo Exercise

We are now going on to styles of pushing hands that involve stepping. These are methods of practicing how to sidestep an attack. Not only that, but they also develop a sense of distance and how to enter into the opponent's sphere. This is an important aspect, as it is due to the practice of these styles of pushing hands that one can blend with, and become part of, the opponent's movement, in a much more active way than the stationary styles of pushing hands. This style of pushing hands is a way of moving outside an attack by stepping out at an angle of 45°. It is a very quick and effective way of dealing with a frontal attack.

1)   2)   3)   4)

1) Starting with the weight on the back foot, the right foot is placed close to the left but with the toes touching the ground. The hands are positioned with the left palm up and the right palm down with the waist turned to the left.

2 - 3) Take a step out to the right at an angle of 45°. This is followed by shifting the weight forward, bringing the left foot in towards the right. At the same time you push forward with the left hand, bringing the right hand back close towards the elbow. This must be done as one coordinated move.

5)   6)   7)

4 - 5) Step out to the left at an angle of 45°. Follow this by stepping in with the right foot and pushing with the right hand, bringing the left hand back, close to the elbow.

6 - 7) Repeat moves 2 - 3.

Partner Exercise

The retreating partner mirrors the forward steps of his partner. The hand movements when retreating are the same as the yielding in the Four Directions Pushing Hands. This style is usually done in a combination of three steps forward and four steps back.

1)   2)   3)   4)

5)   6)   7)

NINE CASTLES PUSH HANDS

1 - 2) Starting with the same posture as in the Four Directions Pushing Hands, take a step across with the left foot, at the same time push forward with the left hand, keeping the right hand by the left elbow. The weight is on the left foot at this point.

3 - 4) Continue by stepping round with the right foot, taking it across the front of the left foot, the weight is then transferred to the right foot. At the same time push forward with the right hand, letting the left hand come back towards the right elbow. Next, step back across with the left foot which takes it back to the starting point, simultaneously turning the waist to the right with the right palm up and the left palm down.

4 - 5) Step back with the right foot, simultaneously turning the waist to the left, with the left palm up and the right palm down.

Nine Castles Pushing Hands
Demonstrated with a Partner

1 - 2) From the starting position in photo 1, take a step across to the right with your left foot, and, at the same time, push straight forward with the left hand. At this point your partner has yielded by shifting his weight back on to the right foot, and turning his waist to the left.

3 - 5) As you step round with your right foot and push with your right hand, your partner steps back with his left foot simultaneously turning his waist to the right. Your partner then steps across with his right foot and pushes forward. At the same time, you sit back neutralising the push by turning to the right. As he steps through and pushes with his left, you step back and turn the waist to the left, the hands adhering to your partner's arm as previously described. The cycle begins again from this point.

To vary the pushing hands practice all you do is reverse the movements. Seven Stars and Nine Castles styles must be practiced countless times so that they become a natural part of your Tai Chi.

THE DA LU SEQUENCE

DA LU

What is shown is the sequence of steps and hand techniques which make up the complete Da Lu style of pushing hands. This style trains stepping and adhering. The eight powers of Tai Chi are incorporated in this method.

THE MARTIAL ART

Tai Chi by definition is a martial art. It is firmly rooted in this tradition. One need only refer to the classics on the art to see how obvious this is.

The martial aspect of Tai Chi is a way of deepening one's understanding of the art. Not to practice this aspect is to miss a great opportunity of giving content to the forms. It should be seen as a way of extending and developing ourselves. The health benefits are enhanced greatly by this practice. Tai Chi as a martial art has, in the past, been neglected in favour of the therapeutic aspect. Although of great worth, it is my belief that the art has been considerably weakened through the emphasis on this apsect. What makes matters worse is that there are those who even deny Tai Chi is a martial art at all. It is a great shame that Tai Chi seems particularly prone to this type of nonsensical thinking.

I feel that Tai Chi for health is too "comfortable" for students to realise their potential, or to benefit fully from the practice. When you begin learning Tai Chi you know nothing of the art. You then begin to learn the hand form. By learning this your potential has increased by that much. If you choose to stop there, then you will gain little in the way of genuine understanding. You must be prepared to keep taking the next step.

APPLICATIONS

To take the next step beyond pushing hands is to learn the self defence aspect of Tai Chi. Exactly the same principles are carried through from pushing hands. For example: if you have to defend against a straight push, the idea is not to wait until the blow is about to land, before responding. By that time the full power of the blow has to be dealt with. Rather, one should meet the attack half way using *softness*. This means that your hand goes out to meet the oncoming limb, *sensing* the direction of the force, *yielding* and diverting the attack into the void. Having done this you maintain contact with your opponent and use an appropriate counter attack. To keep contact, *adhering* is essential to the application of the Tai Chi Chuan techniques. This means you can detect any changes in your opponent's intention and respond in an effective way.

Counters to attacks can take many forms. e.g. punches, kicks, pushes, throws, slaps etc. What is most important is the principle of soft defence (Yin) and hard attack (Yang). The defence is seen as circular while the attacking aspect is seen as square or straight. One should not see these as static positions, as one becomes the other, without any break in continuity. Defence and attack are one.

To deal with an attack invariably involves footwork. This is where the stepping push hands comes into play. Generally, if one is dealing with a straight line attack, you respond by moving to the outside of the line. In this case you would use either the techniques of Seven Stars or Nine Castles. Using any of these styles will take you outside the line of attack at an angle of 45°. This creates a weak line in your opponent's posture through which you can counter. If an attack is coming from the outside you intercept it by going inside. *(see Step Back Repulse Monkey & High Pat The Horse)*

COUNTERING

When you counter there are four elements that combine to make it effective.

1)   *Distance*
You have to develop an understanding of what the correct distance between you and an opponent is. Constant practice of pushing hands will make you aware of this important aspect.

2)   *Angle*
This refers to the angle through which you will attack. If you think of a wheel, with you as the centre, again using the principle of the circle as the defence, the spokes of the wheel are the potential angles of attack. From this you can begin to see how you can create many options from countering.

3)   *Speed*
Things happen with great rapidity in a combat situation, so speed is a crucial element when fighting. Speed for its own sake is of little use, it must be coupled with quality of movement. I believe this comes from initially studying the form and later practicing the practical applications. Taking care in learning the form increases your awareness of how to move, and being able to relax will make the movements economical and smooth.

4)   *Power*
The type of strength used in Tai Chi is of a tensile quality that is springy and whip like which, when used, is focussed for an instant in one direction. There are various ways used to develop this power. The main method is the practice of Internal Strength exercises.

INTERNAL STRENGTH

This aspect consists of two sets of twelve exercises; one Yin and one Yang. The Yin set develops a resilient body, develops coordination and can be beneficial to those of a nervous disposition. The Yang set is more about developing power and physical strength. Although this is the case, it would be foolish to think that it just makes you stronger. It develops a type of tensile strength and will-power that is essential to training in Tai Chi.

These exercises give to Tai Chi the firm internal core which balances the soft external appearance. It is extremely important that these exercises are treated with the utmost respect. If they are not, it is possible to cause injury if they are not properly taught. If they are not fully understood the student will have a very difficult time with little or nothing to show for his efforts. There are three levels to this practice:

Stage One
Harmonising of the external (movement) with the internal (breath).
Stage Two
The mind directs the movements. i.e. the unification of the body and mind.
Stage Three
Enlightenment: where one has insight and has transcended the physical self.

"From the ground up, through the legs, directed by the waist,
up the back, over the shoulders and expressed in the hands."

Coordination is so important. Without it there is a great deal of wasted effort. Coordination also ensures that the whole body is focussed on one point. This isn't just external coordination but one of the mind as well. From the beginning, the hand form is done with both physical and mental focus. This permeates the whole of Tai Chi. It takes time and a lot of patience to progress in the martial aspect of Tai Chi. Your practice must be rooted in reality. Unfortunately, this isn't always the case. Students are too often misled into believing that what they are taught will be effective in application, when in fact there is no substance to what they do. You must know that your techniques will work.

THE TAI CHI PRINCIPLE

The Tai Chi principle is far more important than any specific technique. If you are faced with a situation that has no specific technique, then you must respond by following the Tai Chi principle. In other words, you become one with your opponent's movement and blend with whatever changes take place. To blend with an opponent is to do so in a *spontaneous* way, and not one that requires thought. The time between thought and action is too long, and your responses will be slowed down. *Spontaneity* means that, through your training, you are able to respond in a natural and unforced way. When there is an absence of tension, the response time will be much quicker. You must practice the Tai Chi fighting techniques many thousands of times so they become a reflex action. Here you have an absence of thought, with the mind remaining calm (Yin) in combination with a technique which is a product of thought and development (Yang).

> *"If your opponent doesn't move, you don't move.*
> *If he moves, you move first."*

This saying from the Tai Chi Classics tells you an attack must be dealt with immediately. Using the techniques of sensing and listening, ultimately, an attack can be dealt with before it has really started. Using this concept also means that there is no time to get involved in a prolonged struggle or to indulge in a wrestling bout. Although throws are used in Tai Chi, they should still be seen as ways to deal swiftly with attacks. *You should never resort to brute force.* Combining tensile strength and technique is the correct way.

The idea of becoming the centre of the action, while your opponent is on the periphery is a useful one. This means that you are inside the attack. When attacked by a punch or a kick, it is extremely difficult to catch the hand or the foot, as they are the fastest moving parts. The method is to go behind the hand or foot to the wrist or forearm or the ankle or calf and make them your point of contact.

Using the example of the Tai Chi symbol you can show how the whole concept is used in self-defence. If you have to deal with a straight attack, you are dealing with a Yang force coming towards you. When you meet the attack half way, you are applying small Yin inside the Yang force. As you touch and blend with the attack, you are leading it into nothingness. The strength of the attack has now reached its extreme and becomes Yin. The attack is now at its weakest point. This is the time to counter the attack. This is the application of using softness to overcome hardness.

It is essential not to get stuck in specific techniques. You must be able to flow from one technique to another. Using combinations of techniques will overcome the opponent. Try to go beyond single techniques and see what possibilities can open up. This is also where spontaneity is important. You will become able to sense openings, during an exchange, and have the ability to exploit them

SINGLE WHIP

1) Meet the attack half way by touching his arm. This touch must be soft to detect the force and direction of the attack. At the same time shift the weight back, this will have the effect of leading him forward thus weakening his position.

2) Take hold of his wrist, at the same time turn the waist to the left. This will lead his attack into nothingness (void.)

3) Using Seven Stars stepping move diagonally out to the right, allowing the back foot to follow naturally. You will now be outside his line of attack. Simultaneously striking with the palm of the right hand.

REPULSE MONKEY

1) Using the technique Grasping the Bird's Tail, deflect the opponent's right hand attack by coming inside and deflecting it using the left arm. At the same time the right hand controls the opponent's left arm.

2) Move further inside, at the same time turn the opponent by twisting him, using the right hand to push his shoulder whilst simultaneously pulling with the left hand. This has the effect of creating an angle that allows you to counter through the opponent's weakest point.

3 - 4) Once this position has been achieved the right foot is brought through and sweeps away the opponent's front foot.

TURN THE BODY & SWING FIST

1) When an opponent attacks with a punch to the mid section, use your left forearm to intercept it by going inside the attack. As you touch the arm, at the same time, turn the waist. This leads him into your other hand. This movement leads him into the void and makes him extend himself.

2) Follow this up by using his natural reaction of pulling back, to strike with a backfist counter.

3) Continue by dropping your left hand onto his extended right arm. This allows you to maintain contact with your opponent while following up with a palm strike.

HIGH PAT THE HORSE

1) For an attack from the outside using the technique Grasping the Bird's Tail. Intercept by touching the inside of the arm; at the same time control his right arm by placing the left palm just below the elbow.

2) Follow this up by stepping in placing the right hand at the base of the back. The left hand is placed under the chin.

3) At this point the right hand pulls in towards you and the left hand pushes against the opponent's chin. This is an extremely powerful technique and can be applied with equal effect against a straight attack which is countered from the outside.

BODY FACING LEFT,
KICK IN A CURVE TO THE RIGHT

1 & 2) Intercept the attack by going to meet it; at the same time using the Seven Star method of stepping. This takes you outside the line of attack. Once you have done this immediately turn the waist to the right, kicking in a curve to the opponent's ribs.

STEP BACK TO STRIKE THE TIGER

1) Again the common principle of meeting an attack halfway is shown. Turn the left palm down, pulling your opponent forward.

2) Once this has been achieved continue by turning the waist to the left bringing the right hand onto the opponent's elbow, releasing the left hand to counter.

3) Using the momentum generated by the opponent's force, use the right hand to pull him to the ground.

4) Finish off the technique by striking at the back of the opponent's neck.

SNAKE CREEPS DOWN

1) Meet the attack with both hands.

2) Step back with the right foot and continue to pull him to the ground. The considerable force generated by this pull will have the effect of throwing your opponent to the ground and the momentum will take him past you.

SLAP THE FACE

1) The attack is met halfway by touching the opponent's arm. This deflects the force and direction of the attack.

2) Continue the movement by changing the weight to the back foot, at the same time turning the waist to the left, simultaneously placing the right hand on the opponent's arm. This enables you to re-direct the oncoming force and also maintain contact with your opponent. This technique has the effect of leading your opponent into an unfavourable position.

3) Once you have deflected the attack you counter by using a palm strike to the face. Although there are three stages to the technique, it must be seen as one, with no gaps that could be exploited.

SLAP THE FACE 2

1) This is exactly the same as the previous technique. The difference is that we are now using the Seven Stars style of stepping. As you meet the attack you simultaneously take a step diagonally to the left.

2) Allow the right foot to follow naturally, at the same time, the right hand is preparing to counter.

3) At this point an angle has been created that allows you to counter at the opponent's weakest point.

ELBOW STROKE

1) Lead your opponent's attack by adhering to his attacking arm. As he is extended your left hand meets the back of his head. Again use Seven Stars stepping to take you to the outside of the attack.

2) Shift your weight forward. At the same time bring his head towards you and strike with the elbow.

There are five aspects of the Wudang Tai Chi Chuan system. They are:

Hand Forms
Pushing Hands
Self Defence
Weapons
Internal Strength

For details of classes/seminars contact:

Ian Cameron
Five Winds Tai Chi Chuan
38 Madeira Street
Leith
Edinburgh EH6 4AL
Tel: 0131 554 3947